AYNUK AND AYLI'S BLACK COUNTRY JOKE BOOK

DOUGLAS PARKER

BROADSIDE

THE ORIGINAL "OFF THE CUFF"

BLACK-COUNTRY NIGHT-OUT SHOW

DOLLY ALLEN
HARRY HARRISON
BRIAN CLIFT
JON RAVEN
RAY HINGLEY

**THE HOME GROWN SHOW
THAT FILLS YOUR HALL
AT THE RIGHT PRICE**

**Show Bookings – Contact:
Jon Raven, 68 Limes Road, Tettenhall,
Wolverhampton. Tel. W'ton 753047/741536**

First published in Great Britain by Broadside in 1984.

ISBN 0 946757 02 X

Printed in Great Britain by
Cox and Wyman Limited,
Cardiff Road, Reading, Berkshire.

Front cover design John Crane.

Set in Times by
JH Graphics Limited, Reading

Broadside
Studley House,
68 Limes Road,
Tettenhall, Wolverhampton

LET'S BOST OFF! 5

Aynuk: "What's the difference between a buffalo and a bison?"

Ayli: "I doh know, I've never washed me hands in a buffalo."

A little chap had been out for the day with his father. When he got home his mother asked, "Well, did yo 'av a good time at the zoo?"

"Smashing," said the lad. "And Dad wore arf chuffed when one of the animals cum racing in at forty to one."

Aynuk says they doh 'av a village idiot in Cradley. He reckons they teck it in turns.

Ayli was late for work and the gaffer asked him where he had been. Ayli said, "I've been to 'av me hair cut."

Gaffer: "In the firms time?"

Ayli: "Well it grows in the firms time, doh it?"

Gaffer: "It doh all grow in the firms time!"

Ayli: "I day 'av it all cut off."

6

What do you call a Chinaman who lives between Stourbridge and Cradley Heath?
Yo min Lye.

Aynuk and Ayli were working on the building site.
Aynuk: "Cum on our Ayli, wot about fetchin' sum more bricks?"
Ayli: "I ay well our Aynuk. I'm tremblin' from head to foot."
Aynuk: "In that case yo'd better get workin' wi' the sieve."

Aynuk was crawling across the desert thinking it was the last time he would go on a Midland Red mystery tour. His eyes were glazed in the hot sun as his parched voice cried, "I'm lost . . . water! I'm lost!"

As he squinted into the sunlight he could just see his mate, Ayli, dressed in eskimo fur. He was riding a sledge, pulled by a team of huskies, over the sand dunes.

"Mush, mush!" shouted Ayli as he drove forward until he finally drew up alongside Aynuk who glanced up and cried, "Help me . . . I'm lost!"

Ayli paused to adjust his snowshoe and said, *"Yo'm lost!"*

7

A chap dashed into the pub and shouted, "Quick, give us a pint afore the trouble starts."

The landlord gave him a pint and the chap swigged it down.

"Give us another, quick, afore the trouble starts."

Another pint goes down and the landlord says, "What's all this about trouble starting?"

"Well," says the chap, "I ay got no money!"

Another chap runs into a pub and shouts, "Watch out, Big Sid's back in town and he's lookin' for trouble."

In seconds everyone runs out of the pub and the landlord is left staring at an empty room. Moments later the door opens with a mighty thud and in walks a giant of a man. His granite like chin is covered in stubble. Enormous muscles ripple beneath his shirt. He thumps the bar, "Quick barman, give me a whisky."

The landlord, trembling, gives him a drink which the stranger gulps down in one swig.

"D – d – d – do you want another?" asks the landlord.

"I ay got time," comes the reply, "I've heard Big Sid's back in town and he's looking for trouble!"

Aynuk reckons his missus is so saft 'er thinks Dudley Port is a new type of dinner wine.

8

The small child was asked to describe a funeral.
"Well," he said, "it's jus' like a weddin' . . .
only wi' a box!"

*There's someat evil about Black Country kids
sometimes. A little lad returned from school in a
hell of a mess, blazer torn, nose blooded, knees
grazed.*

*"It was my own fault," he told his father. "I
challenged Tommy Riley to a duel and gave him a
choice of weapons."*

"What did he choose?" asked his dad.

*The boys eyes fell to the floor as he murmured,
"His big sister."*

A chap was standing in the butchers when a large
dog ran in and stole a joint of meat. As the dog
ran off down the street the butcher shouted,
"Hey, that's your dog, ain't it?"

The chap looked at the ceiling and casually
replied, "Well he used to be but he fends for
'imself now."

"This ere comprehensive educashun ay doing our nipper no good."

"What meks yer say that?"

"They told 'im to spell taerters wi' a 'P'!"

A lecturer at the Royal Hospital was testing one of his pupils.

"You can see from this X-ray that this patient has one leg shorter than the other which is the reason that he limps. Tell me, what would you do in a case like this?"

The pupil thought for a moment then replied, "I think, sir, that I should limp too."

In Cradley Heath they've all got great hairy arms and legs with big muscles. They chew tobacco and have big black moustaches . . . and you should see the men!

10

BLACK COUNTRY DUCK

"Personally, I blames the parents!"

Ayli got a job with the corporation. He worked for the refuse disposal department and soon got the hang of the job. He was so good he could carry a bin under each arm whilst balancing another on his head. Then off he'd go, whistling while he worked.

Aynuk said, "That's fantastic, Ayli, how dun yo do it?"

Ayli: "Easy, mate, I just puts me lips together and blows!"

Aynuk: "Is your missus from Norway?"
Ayli: "No, mate, 'er just looks like an 'orse."

Ayli went along to a parents night at his nippers school. "How's our Tommy comin' on?" he asked the teacher.

"Well," came the reply, "he's in a class of his own."

Ayli was chuffed. "I day know 'e was that clever."

"Oh he's not," said the teacher, "but he smells!"

12

Aynuk went along to the building site looking for a job. The foreman asked him if he could work with a wheelbarrow. "Sorry mate," he says, "I ay no good wi' machinery!"

While he was there he saw his mate Ayli running up and down a ladder with a load of bricks.
"Yo'll be worn out wi' all that work," says Aynuk
"Doh yo fret," says Ayli, "I've got 'em fooled. I'm using the same bricks every time."

A couple of hundred years ago two Black Country chaps were hacking their way through the jungle (probably on an 18–30 holiday) when suddenly they saw a strange looking beast with a horn on its nose standing in the clearing.
"Why doh we call that a Rhinoceros," said one.
"Why?" said the other.
"'Cos it looks more like a Rhinoceros than anything else we've seen yet!"

Aynuk and Ayli were in a cafe looking at the menu.
Aynuk: "I wonder what this 'ere 'soup of the day' is like."
Ayli: "It's lovely, mate, I 'ad sum yesterday in London."

Aynuk and Ayli were chatting. Ayli reckoned that true friends such as they should share and share alike.

"Yo mean," said Aynuk, "if yo 'ad two 'ouses yo would gi' me one?"

"Course I 'ud," said Ayli.

"And if yo 'ad two cars?" said Aynuk.

"I'd gi' yo one," said Ayli.

"Wot if yo 'ad two pigs?" said Aynuk.

"That ay fair," said Ayli, "yo know I've got two pigs!"

Aynuk: "The missus 'ad plastic surgery last week."
Ayli: "Painful was it?"
Aynuk: "Ar, I cut off her credit card."

Aynuk and Ayli went to a funeral in Lye. They'd had a few (well he would have wanted it that way, wouldn't he?) and when they went to look in the coffin they lifted up the piano lid by mistake.

"I cor remember who 'e was, said Aynuk, "but he 'ad a bostin' set of teeth."

"Ar," said Ayli, "but he'd had hell of a lot of fillings!"

14

Aynuk: "I call the missus 'Wonder woman'."

Ayli: "Why's that, mate?"

Aynuk: "'Cos I sometimes wonder if 'er is a woman! Mind yo 'ers med me think more about religion."

Ayli: "In what way?"

Aynuk: "Well I day believe in hell 'til I married 'er!"

Ayli was watching two kids in the street. One kid held his hand in front of a wall and invited the other child to hit it as hard as he liked. So the child threw a terrific punch at the hand which the first kid moved at the last moment. This caused the other child to hit the wall with his fist and he ran off down the street bawling his eyes out.

Later that night Ayli met Aynuk and couldn't wait to show him the 'trick' he'd learnt.

"Goo on then," said Aynuk.

"Well," said Ayli holding his hand up in front of his face. "First yo've got to hit me hand as 'ard as yo con!"

Aynuk reckons Ayli is so saft he thinks the Charge of the Light Brigade is an electricity bill.

He reckons Ayli has sold his telly to buy a video and he caught him looking in the paper to find out when the 9 o'clock news was on.

Aynuk was in court after a bit of domestic trouble.

"You're no stranger here," said the judge. "Fighting with the wife, indeed. Liquor again?"

"No I day," replied Aynuk, rubbing his head, "'er licked me!"

Aynuk and Ayli decided to take up snooker and since neither had played before they figured it would be best to play against each other until they were good enough to tackle other opposition.

First time on the table they had been playing for about an hour and, although neither had potted a ball, had thoroughly enjoyed themselves. However, in the interest of getting the game finished before the club closed, Aynuk sidled up to Ayli and whispered, "Quick, while nobody's lookin' – tek that wooden triangle off the table!"

Aynuk says that to save water during the summer drought they closed three lanes of Brierley Hill swimming baths!

16

Aynuk: "I'm mekin' a cabinet for the missus. How do I know whether to use a screw or a nail?"

Ayli: "That's easy, mate. Yo drive in a nail and if the wood splits yo should 'ave used a screw."

A chap in the pub was boasting about his dog. It was back in the days when blokes would let two dogs fight and take side bets on which one would win.

"Aynuks dog 'ud see 'im off," said Ayli.

The chap was not convinced and accepted a five pound wager that his bull terrier could fight Aynuks and win. So off went Ayli and returned half an hour later with Aynuk and his 'champion'.

"E's a funny lookin' 'un," said the challenger.

"Doh yo worry 'e can fight like a good 'un," said Aynuk.

He was right. The two animals were put together and in less than a minute the bull terrier was done for.

"Well yo're dog con certainly fight. Never seen such a savage beast afore. Mind, I still think e's a funny lookin' dog."

"Ar 'e is," agreed Aynuk, "and he was even funnier afore I shaved off 'is mane!"

Aynuk to new vicar in the Parish.

"I'm glad yo've cum vicar. We day know what sin was 'til yo arrived."

17

"What di yo 'av for yer birthday?"
"I day get nuthin."
"Ow cum?"
"Well I asked me muther for an encyclopaedia and 'er said as I could walk to school like the other kids!"

The solicitor was reading Aynuks will to the gathered will wishers all eager for a share in his estate. He read the final paragraph, "I always said I would mention my dear pal, Ayli, in my will. So without further ado, Hello there Ayli!"

Aynuk and Ayli were in the Art gallery looking at a bit of culture. They spent some time considering a large abstract painting.
"Well," said Aynuk, "I've often 'ad 'angover but that's the fust time I've seen a picture of one!"

18

Aynuk took up with this landscape gardening business and was working at a posh house. He was busily engaged on a rockery but he would stop working every ten minutes or so and walk over to the garden wall. After much tut tutting to himself he would shake his head and shout, "Green side up!"

After a couple of hours of this the lady of the house went into the garden to inspect his handywork.

"It's coming along nicely," she said, "but tell me, what's all this 'Green side up' business?"

"Yo'll 'ave to bear with me, missus," said Aynuk, "I've got our Ayli next door layin' turf!"

Ayli was counting sheep in a field.

"One, two, three, four, another one, and another . . ."

"Our father must 'ave bin in the police orchestra."

"What meks yer say that?"

"Well they keep cumin' round askin' where he's hidden the lute."

Aynuk: "The doctor reckons I've got high blood pressure."

Ayli: "Oh ar, is it bad?"

Aynuk: "Well he says that if I day 'av skin I'd be a fountain."

The Bishops were competing to see who could ordain the most priests in the shortest time.
The record was 45 revs. per minute.

Aynuk: "Want to buy this genuine skull of Shakespeare?"

Ayli: "But yo sold me Shakespeare's skull last week and it wore as big as that."

Aynuk: "Ar but that was the skull of Shakespeare as a boy."

Ayli: "My missus says that if it's true about reincarnation she wouldn't mind comin' back as a pig or a cow."

Aynuk: "What did yo say?"

Ayli: "I told 'er that's no good 'cos yo av to come back as someat different."

20

BLACK COUNTRY DUCK

"He doh arf get touchy if yo say 'nice weather fer ducks'!"

Hear about the saft chap who hijacked an escalator in Woolworths and demanded to be taken to Marks and Spencer.

Aynuk: "What am yo mekin' wi' that wood?"
Ayli: "A portable."
Aynuk: "A portable what?"
Ayli: "I doh know yet, I've only med the 'andle."

Aynuk goes to see Ayli to borrow a file.

"What dun yo want if for?" asks Ayli.

"My budgie has gorra corn on 'is yed and I'm gonna file it off," says Aynuk.

"Doh be so saft," says Ayli. "Yo'll kill it."

"No I wo," says Aynuk, "I'll do it gentle." So off he goes.

The following day he sees Ayli who asks him about the budgie.

"Oh he's jed," says Aynuk.

"There yo am," says Ayli, "I said the file ud kill 'im."

"It wor that," says Aynuk "I think I 'ad 'im in the vice too tight."

22

Ayli: "I'm feelin' proper depressed mate."
Aynuk: "Why's that our kid?"
Ayli: "Well I sent away £35 three weeks ago to join the A.A. and I haven't 'ad me motorbike and uniform yet."

The teacher had just read the story of Jonah and the whale.

"Now Tommy, what does the story tell you?" she asked.

"Well, miss," said Tommy, "it shows yo' cor keep a good mon down."

The same teacher tried again, this time with the parable of the prodigal son.

"Now Tommy, who was not pleased to see the prodigal son return?" she asked.

Quick as a flash Tommy replied. "The fatted calf!"

Aynuk: "How many hundredths are there in an inch?"
Ayli: "Cor, there must be thousands, mate!"

23

Aynuk and Ayli were out in eskimo land, somewhere south of Smethwick, sailing along the cut in a kayak. It became very cold. Cold enough to freeze the faggots off a brass fender. They were so cold that Ayli made a fire on the bottom of the kayak which was soon engulfed in flames and they had to swim to the edge of the cut for safety.

"I cor understand why the kayak burnt like that," said Ayli.

"It just goes to prove," said Aynuk. "Yo cor 'ave yer Kayak and 'eat it!"

Aynuk: "How do yo stop moles diggin' in the garden?"
Ayli: "Hide all the shovels."

Aynuk: "My mother-in-law is like one of them Exocet missiles."
Ayli: "How do yer mean?"
Aynuk: "Well yo know it's gonna cum but there's nowt yo can do about it."

24

Aynuk saw Ayli struggling up the road with a couple of builders hods under his arms and a hen perched on each one of them.

"What am yo a doing, our Ayli," said Aynuk.

"It's for the missus," said Ayli, "when 'er knew I was going up to town 'er asked me to bring back one or two 'ods and 'ens."

There's a fellow in Gornal who is so lazy that when his missus asked him to go out and see if it was raining, replied, "Why doh yo call the dog in and see if he's wet?"

After seeing the sign in the big store, 'Dogs must be carried up the escalator', Aynuk spent three hours trying to find a dog!

Aynuk: "Yo look a bit down in the mouth, mate."
Ayli: "Ar, I've lost me dog and I cor find him nowhere."
Aynuk: "Why doh yo put an ad in the paper?"
Ayli: "Doh be saft, our dog cor read."

A big variety agent was passing a building site when he saw Aynuk do two double somersaults, a back flip off the cement mixer and land on his feet.

"I'd like to book him," said the agent.

"Yo'd better book his mate, Ayli, an all," said the gaffer.

"Why?" said the agent.

"Cos he's the chap that hit 'is hand wi' the sledghommer."

Ayli went into the newsagent and asked for a paper.

Newsagent: "Do you want todays or tomorrows?"

Ayli thought for a moment then said, "I'll have tomorrows."

"Okay," said the newsagent. "Come back in the morning."

The next day Ayli went in for his paper.

Newsagent: "They're going up in price tomorrow.

Ayli, not wishing to get caught out again, said, "In that case I'll take a dozen!"

26

After years of doing the pools Aynuk had had no success. Then one day there was a knock at the door. Aynuk answered it, because he was bright like that, and a smart fellow was standing on the doorstep.

"I'm from Littlewoods," he said.

"Yo doh mean ter say I've won the pools?" cried Aynuk.

"No," replied the chap. "We've just caught yer missus shoplifting!"

Aynuk: "I've found out the secret of long life."
Ayli: "What's that, mate?"
Aynuk: "Getting married."
Ayli: "Yo mean ter say that gettin' married makes you live longer?"
Aynuk: "No mate, but it sure seems like it."

Aynuk: "I took the dog to the vets today because it bit the missus."
Ayli: "Did yo 'ave 'im put down?"
Aynuk: "No mate, I 'ad 'is teeth sharpened!"

Aynuk had a butchers shop and he employed Ayli to do odd jobs, like hanging the mince and weighing the legs of liver. (I told you they were odd jobs.) Ayli noticed a sign in the window which read 'Chicken sausages 50p a pound.'

Ayli: "Ow can yo sell chicken sausages at that price, our kid?"

Aynuk: "Well doh tell nobody but I do put in a bit of hoss meat. Mind yo, I am fair, Ayli. Fifty-fifty, one hoss—one chicken."

The school inspector put a question to the class. "Who wrote Macbeth?"

Little Tommy Baker, who was always in trouble, said, "It wor me, sir!"

The inspector was apalled at the standard of Black Country education. He marched into the Headmasters office and told the story. Fuming, he said, "Tommy Baker actually said it wasn't him!"

"Well," remarked the headmaster, "I know Tommy and if he says he didn't write it I'm inclined to believe him."

Aynuk was amazed to see Ayli hobbling up the street on crutches with both ankles in plaster.

"Yo'm in a state and that's fer sure, what's bin doing?" he asked.

"I've learnt my lesson," says Ayli, "that's the last time I meks me own cocunut wine."

28

"I was just considerin'," said Ayli. "If I 'ad a job I reckon I'd like to be Father Christmas."

"Ows that?" said Aynuk

"Well," said Ayli, "he doh 'ave to shave and 'e only works one day a year."

Two hundred employees walked out of a Black Country steelmill during production hours after being told by their union that it was best to strike while the iron was hot.

Aynuk was called up for the army but he didn't want to go. So he claimed he had very poor eyesight and made sure that he failed all the normal tests. He was delighted when he was rejected and went straight to the cinema to celebrate. He hadn't been in his seat five minutes when in walked his examiner who immediately recognised him. Quick as a flash Aynuk said, "Am I on the right bus for Cradley?"

29

A little lad went home feeling really excited that he'd been chosen for the school play. He told his father, "I've got the role of an old married man."

His father patted him on the head sympathetically. "Never mind son," he said, "maybe next year you'll get a speaking part."

A Kleptomaniac went to see his doctor and on his return home his wife enquired how he had faired.

"I've gorra tek these tablets three times a day and if I ay no better by Tuesday the doc's asked me to get him a colour telly."

Two Black Country kids were paddling in the sea at Rhyl.

"Yo're feet ay arf dirty," said the first.

"They've every right to be," said the other, "we day cum last year."

30

BLACK COUNTRY DUCK

"He ay bin the same since 'e sid the Synchronised Swimming in the Olympics!"

Then there was the Black Country burglar. His wife wanted a gold necklace for her birthday so he threw a brick into the jewellers window and got one for her. Then at Christmas she was pestering him for a mink coat. He threw a brick into a furriers window and once again she was happy.

Recently she's been pestering him for a gold watch but he's put his foot down. He said, "I doh get no peace. 'Er must think as I'm med of bricks."

Aynuk was driving along in his old car when he got a puncture. He jumped out and jacked the old banger up so that he could fix the spare. After a few minutes a chap strolled over and casually lifted the car bonnet.

"What do yo think yo'm doing?" shouted Aynuk.

"Fairs fair," said the chap. "If yo'm 'avin the wheels I'm 'avin the battery!"

Ayli: "I've just bought a new suit and paid extra for two pairs of trousers."

Aynuk: "That'll last yer for ages."

Ayli: "I doh think so, I've just burnt 'ole in the jacket!"

32

Aynuk hasn't always disliked his mother-in-law. When she first moved in with him he said. "Remember, my 'ouse is your 'ouse."

So she sold it.

Aynuk says, "There was a hell of a row when the council found out!"

There have been some hard times in the Black Country. Aynuk never bothers to vote in the elections these days. He reckons its like changing deckchairs on the Titanic.

There was a massive funeral in Wolverhampton. About twenty thousand walked behind the hearse. All nationalities were there to pay their respects.

Aynuk: "Must 'ave bin an important bloke."

Ayli: "Ar 'e was the Social Security Officer."

Aynuk: "People always say as Black Country folk is thick, doh 'em?"

Ayli: "They do mate."

Aynuk: "Well I read in the paper as 'ow the population of London is the densest in the whole country."

Policeman to Black Countryman after a fight.

"Could you describe your assailant?"

"That's what I were doing when 'e thumped me!"

Aynuk and Ayli were sat in the pub, supping. Ayli's eyes were fixed on an antelopes head which had been mounted on the wall.

"I was just a thinkin'," said Ayli, "that animal must 'ave bin going at 'ell of a speed when 'e it that wall!"

Some say Aynuk has got holes in his face from where he was learning to eat with a fork.

Ayli reckons its because his mother fed him frozen peas with a catapult . . . and missed his gob!

Aynuk says, "Me and the missus have been married for forty years. There's nowt I wouldn't do for 'er and there's nowt 'er wouldn't do for me. And that's what we do for each other . . . nowt!"

34

Aynuk: "I'm going to buy the missus a present that's really useful."

Ayli: "Ar, but will yo get 'er to wear a muzzle?"

Aynuk: "It's doubtful, mate, 'er woh use that electric chair I bought 'er for Christmas."

Ayli: "No sense of humour sum women."

Aynuk: "I even offered to ask your missus to 'old 'er hand while we tried it out."

Ayli: "Yo've allus bin a good mate ter me an that's fer sure."

Aynuk: "Ar, I remember on yer wedding day when the vicar asked who was going to give the bride away."

Ayli: "Yo said that yo could but yo'd bin paid to keep yer gob shut."

Aynuk: "Loff? I thought they'd never start."

Ayli: "'Ers never forgiven yer yo know."

Aynuk: "No sense of humour sum women!"

Heard about Aynuks war wound. Apparently a car backfired in the blackout and he pulled a muscle running to the air raid shelter.

Mind you he did his bit for King and Country. He was in France when the first gun was fired . . . and in Cradley when the second went off!

When Aynuk was called up for active service he didn't want to go. Even at the medical he complained, "I ay no good for the army. Me nerves is bad. If anyone shouts at me I jumps."

"Right," said the Medical Officer, "Paratroopers!"

Aynuk: "I'm thinkin' of buying one of them nuclear fall-out shelters."
Ayli: "They're expensive, mate, why doh yer 'ang on a bit and gerra second hand one?"

The vicar had unnerved everyone at Aynuks marriage ceremony by arriving late. Years passed and he met the bridegroom again and greeted him enthusiastically. "Well," said the priest, "it's been nearly twenty years since I gave you that awful fright at your wedding."

"Ar," replied Aynuk ruefully, "and I've still got 'er!"

Aynuk: "I ay spoken to the missus fer six months . . . I doh like to interrupt 'er!"
Ayli: "Well my missus talks through 'er nose . . . I think 'er mouth has worn out!"

36

The young couple were sitting on a bench in the moonlight. She looked lovingly into his eyes and murmured, "Darling, will you still love me when I'm old?"

He held her hand tenderly and replied, "I will love you when rivers cease to flow, when stars no longer shine and the sun forgets to kiss the morning . . . but yo wo' end up lookin' like yer mother will yer?"

Aynuk was doing a competition in the paper.

"Can yo name five animals that cum from Africa?" he asked Ayli.

Ayli scratched his head, then with a burst of inspiration, "An elephant . . . and four giraffes!"

When Ayli caught the bus he noticed that the time by the church clock was 10.15. A little later on he caught sight of another church clock which showed 10.05. So he got off the bus because he thought he must be going the wrong way.

Aynuk: "Did yo enjoy that seacruise yo went on?"

Ayli: "Ar it were great."

Aynuk: "And them tablets the doc' give yer for sea sickness, did they work?"

Ayli: "Ar I was sick twice."

Aynuk: "Had some rough seas then?"

Ayli: "Oh ar, but the Captain come down and give us lifeboat drill. He kept shoutin' 'women and children first' I doh think he was being really fair."

Aynuk: "Wot meks yo say that?"

Ayli: "Well he was wearing a chiffon frock at the time!"

Aynuk: "I bet yo couldn't keep a straight face."

Ayli: "No mate, I loffed so much I very nearly dropped me 'andbag."

Aynuk: "But was it a well kept ship?"

Ayli: "Ar, the Captain said all the crew was hand picked and he could trust everyone of 'em wi' his life."

Aynuk: "That must 'ave impressed yer?"

Ayli: "Ar until I saw one of the deckhands, who was swabbing, suddenly washed overboard by a giant wave!"

Aynuk: "That 'ud spoil yer 'oliday. Wot did yer do?"

Ayli: "I told the Captain that one of the crew who 'e thought 'e could trust wi' his life 'ad just cleared off wi' his mop and bucket!"

38

Aynuk went round to see Ayli's new dog which kept barking and leaping up at him as he walked up the path.

"My word 'e doh 'arf bark some," said Aynuk.

"Yes," said Ayli, "but you know the saying 'a barking dog never bites'?"

"Ar," said Aynuk, "I know the saying and yo know the saying but does yo'r dog know it?"

The Duke of Edinburgh was on a tour of a Black Country factory and paused to chat with a chap who was sweeping up. He soon realised that the labourer was unhappy because he was a skilled bricklayer and had in fact built his own house single-handed.

"But," said the chap, "they won't give me a skilled job 'ere just 'cos I day pass the intelligence test."

The Duke was appalled by this and promised to have a word with the bosses before he left the premises.

Half an hour later, as he was walking across the yard to the offices, a housebrick whizzed passed the Duke, narrowly missing his head. He looked round to see the smiling face of the labourer shouting, "Yo wo' forget will yer!"

Aynuk: "How long does it tek to get from 'ere to Lye?"

Ayli: "It's about a ten minute walk if yo run like hell."

A bailiff went to a house in the Black Country to serve a summons. He didn't know that the occupier was hiding behind the door with a pair of bellows. When the bailiff posted the summons the chap inside blew it back out under the door. The bailiff tried again and the same thing happened. So back to the Town Hall went the official. "I didn't get the rent," he said, "and I wouldn't pay it either if I lived in a house that draughty!"

Ayli was playing bingo and getting a bit excited because he only had a couple of numbers to get.

"Key of the door . . . twenty-one!" shouted the caller.

Ayli crossed it off and held his breath.

"Unlucky for some . . ."

"House!" shouted Ayli.

"Number twelve," continued the caller.

"Eh, mate," says Ayli, a bit upset, "twelve ay an unlucky number."

"It is for you," came the reply.

Aynuk had lost his missus so he went to the police station with Ayli to report her missing.

Aynuk: "'Ers a nicely rounded woman, fair haired, good looking, someat like Felicity Kendal."

Ayli: "Hang on mate, your missus ay nuthing like that."

Aynuk: "I know that yer fule, but who the hell wants her back?"

40

BLACK COUNTRY DUCK

"Just 'cos I mentioned I'd got turkey sandwiches fer lunch!"

There's something about Black Country kids.

"Is your mother in?" the salesman asked the small boy who was playing in the garden.

"Ar 'er is," said the little chap.

The salesman knocked the door, waited, knocked the door again . . . but still no reply.

"I thought you said your mother was in," he said to the lad.

"'Er is," came the reply, "but this ay our house."

Aynuk and Ayli were out playing golf.
Ayli: "Yo know it's my birthday. Wot am yo gonna give me?"
Aynuk paused, then, "I'll gi' yo the next two holes."

Aynuk and Ayli won a fortune on the pools so they went out on the town to celebrate. First stop was a posh restaurant. No expense spared . . . they even had soup. Ayli was a bit puzzled by all the different knives and forks but Aynuk said it was probably because they had more than one sitting so they took no notice and carried on. The waiter even kept a discreet silence when Ayli drank the finger bowl.

At the end of the meal Aynuk insisted on settling the bill. On the way home they passed a car showroom and their eyes were out on stalks looking at the gleaming Rolls-Royce's.

"I tell yer wot," said Ayli, "we'll have one each. But I'm paying for these, Aynuk, after all yo paid for the meal."

42

A chap flew over British Leyland at Longbridge taking aerial photographs. One of the pictures didn't come out. Somebody on the production line must have moved!

Aynuk and Ayli bought a tandem and went on a cycling holiday in Wales. One hill was particularly steep and our two heroes were well spent by the time they got to the top. It was five minutes before Aynuk could speak but when he got his breath he said, "I thought that one 'ad got us beat. I ay never seen an 'ill so steep."

"Yo'm right," said Ayli. "We might 'ave slipped back down if I 'adn't kept the brakes on."

Aynuk and Ayli in the pub.

Ayli: "Doh drink no more, mate, yo've 'ad enough."

Aynuk: "'Ow do yer mek that out, I ay drunk."

Ayli: "Yo must be, yer face is gerrin' blurred already."

43

Aynuk tried to get a job at a local factory but was told that there was no work available.

"Yo could tek me on," he insisted. "The bit I do wouldn't even be noticed."

Aynuk: "Where 'av yo bin, Ayli?"
Ayli: "I've just taken me new tie back to the shop."
Aynuk: "Why, day yo like the colour?"
Ayli: "It wor that . . . it was too tight."

Aynuk and Ayli went on a plane for the first time in their lives.

Aynuk was a bit worried and says to Ayli, "It' 'ud be awful if we fell out!"

"Doh be saft," says Ayli, "we've been pals for years."

Ayli: "I keeps on getting pains in me yed, mate."
Aynuk: "I never 'as that trouble. I allus 'ave a drop of whisky about an hour afore I feels any pain comin' on."

44

Aynuk was working on the buses as a conductor. He went upstairs to collect the fares and there were two nuns looking a little perturbed.

One of the nuns said, "I'm sorry we've forgotten the money for our fares but we'll give you our names and addresses. We're both Sisters of John the Baptist."

"You must think I'm saft," said Aynuk, "John the Baptist is dead."

Aynuk went to the big city and came across a posh restaurant which claimed that they could serve any meal requested.

"I'll soon catch this lot out," he thought as he took his seat and promptly ordered an elephants trunk on toast.

The waiter looked terribly embarrassed.

"I bet I've caught yo lot out ay I?" laughed Aynuk.

"I'm afraid you have, sir," came the reply, "we've run out of bread."

So Aynuk went to work on a building site. The gaffer asked him to dig a hole thirty feet deep, twenty feet wide and fifty feet long.

"Doh be saft," said Aynuk. "It 'ud be the death of me."

"We'll give you a J.C.B.," said the gaffer.

"Yo can keep yer medals," replied Aynuk, "I still ay doing it."

Nor 'e day!

Ayli went to buy a piece of wrapping paper 1 inch by 50 yards so that he could send a new clothes line to his mother.

His mother had to send the line back because her garden wasn't long enough.

Ayli: "I ay bin feelin' well mate."
Aynuk: "Dun yo 'ave any trouble passing water?"
Ayli: "No, but I feel a bit giddy when I crosses a bridge."

Aynuk: "I was readin' as 'ow in the jungle the tempreture is over 100 degrees, even in the middle of the night."

Ayli: "And I bet it's just as bad in the shade?"

Aynuk went into a cafe. The sign on the counter read 'Food at popular prices'.

"I'll have faggots and peas," said Aynuk.

"That will be six quid," said the owner.

"Six quid for faggots and peas. I thought yo sold food at popular prices!"

"Well," said the owner, "I like 'em."

46

Aynuk had been having trouble sleeping and he mentioned this to his mate, Ayli.

"I 'ad that problem," said Ayli, "but the doc' gid me some pills and I 'ad a smashing nights sleep. I used to dream I was in Tesco's surrounded by polite cashiers. All beautiful girls helping me wi' me shopping and asking me out after work."

Not surprisingly Aynuk went off to the doctors and asked him for the same treatment. Within a couple of days he was back complaining.

"Them pills yo gid Ayli med him 'ave wonderful dreams but all I get is 'orrible nightmares about coming out of Asda wi' no change in me pocket. Why can't I 'ave nice dreams like Ayli?"

"Well," replied the doctor, "Ayli is a private patient. You are only National Health."

Aynuk: "What am yo going to call yer new nipper?"
Ayli: "The missus thought of callin' him John."
Aynuk: "I wouldn't if I was yo. Every Tom, Dick and Harry is called John these days."

Aynuk and Ayli went to the pictures to see a western.

Aynuk: "I bet yo a quid as that cowboy falls off is 'oss when 'e rides into town."

Ayli: "Yo'm on mate."

So they sit and wait and sure enough the cowboy fell off his horse when he rode into town.

Aynuk: "There yo am, mate, that's a quid yo owe me. I cor tell a lie though, I knew as 'e would fall off 'cos I've seen the film afore."

Ayli: "So 'ave I but I day think he'd be saft enough to do it again."

Ayli: *"My missus reckons I should see a psychiatrist."*

Aynuk: *"Wot did yo say?"*

Ayli: *"I told 'er that anyone who is daft enough to go to a psychiatrist should 'ave 'is yed examined!"*

Aynuk: "I hear yo 'ad to pay fifty quid to 'ave yer car towed to a garage?"

Ayli: "Ar, I thought 'e was overchargin' me so I kept me handbrake on all the way to mek him earn it!"

48

Some years ago Aynuk decided to put himself forward in the local elections. He soon found out that not everyone was interested in his point of view.

"I wouldn't vote for you if you were the Archangel Gabriel!" shouted one woman with ferocity.

Aynuk didn't bat an eyelid.

"If I was the Archangel Gabriel, missus, yo wouldn't be in my constituency."

Ayli: "This watch I bought up town is a belter."
Aynuk: "Wot meks it so special."
Ayli: "Well, it does an hour in forty minutes!"

Ayli: "I've med a fool of British Rail."
Aynuk: "'Ows that?"
Ayli: "I've bought a return ticket to Wolverhampton and I ay comin back!"

Little chap at school has been learning the Alphabet.

Teacher: "Now Johnny, what comes after T?"

Johnny: "The six o' clock news, miss."

Aynuk: "What's illegal mean?"

Ayli: "I dunno, is it a sick bird?"

Ayli: "We 'ad a smashin' holiday."

Aynuk: "What was the digs like?"

Ayli: "Proper posh, wi' them luvly big fluffy towels."

Aynuk: "Gerra way."

Ayli: "It's right, I 'ad hell of a game shutting me suitcases when we cum home!"

Aynuk went for a job down the mines. The gaffer said, "Do you know your gas regulations?"

Aynuk says, "Well I know it's mark 7 for Yorkshire pudding!"

50

BLACK COUNTRY DUCK

"'E's going through one of 'is insecure periods!"

51

"What's up wi' yo?" Aynuk asked his missus. "Yo only talked for twenty minutes on the 'phone."

"I know," said his wife, "I gorra wrong number."

Ayli had not been well. His doctor said it was the booze and limited him to one a day.
  So far he's up to April 16th, 1996.

Aynuk. "Is it yo that's puttin' it about that I'm stupid?"
Ayli: "Well I day know it was a secret."

Ayli: "I cum out of the 'ouse the other day and saw a chap mekin' off wi' me car."
Aynuk: "Did yo manage to catch 'im?"
Ayli: "No, but I got his number."

52

Aynuk was trying one of those quizzes in the paper.

"Dun yo know what a widower is?" he asked Ayli.

"Ar," came the swift reply, "the husband of a widow."

Aynuk and Ayli were chatting again. This time about love.

Aynuk: "Yo see, mate, I'm in love wi' two women. The one is a stunner, really nice to look at but 'er ay got no money. Now the other ay so grand, a bit plain but 'er comes from a very rich family."

Ayli: "Yo be ruled by me, our Aynuk. I think that deep down yo really care fer the beautiful lass. You goo ahead and marry 'er."

Aynuk: "Yo'm a good mate an' that's fer sure. I'll be on my way to her house."

Ayli: "Afore yo goo, I doh suppose yo could gi' me the address of the other wench."

Aynuk: "What would yo do if yo broke yer arm in two places?"

Ayli: "I wouldn't go back to them two places again."

53

Aynuk went to Canada and saw a couple of chaps cutting down trees using a cross-cut saw. A small chap was pulling at one end and a big feller was pulling at the other. After watching for a while Aynuk went up to the big man and said, "Doh be such a bully. If the little chap wants to use the saw yo should let 'im 'ave it!"

Ayli was also a man of principle. There was the time when he was insulted by a man seated in the lounge of the local hostelry. Ayli had accidentally spilled a glass of beer over the chap who reacted by calling him all the names under the sun. Ayli felt his Black Country pride swell beneath his jacket.

"That's fightin' talk where I cum from," he shouted.

"Oh it is, is it?" the man responded as he stood up to reveal a frame which was well over six foot tall.

"Yes," gulped Ayli, nervously, "only I doh live there now."

54

Aynuk: "The doctor told me I only had two weeks to live."

Ayli: "Wot did yo say?"

Aynuk: "I asked him if I could 'ave the last week in July and the fust in August."

Ayli: "Yo should av gone for a second opinion. If he'd given yer two weeks as well yo would 'av 'ad a month."

Aynuk: "'Ow yo gerrin' on wi' that new electric cooker?"

Ayli: "It's fantastic, I've 'ad it for six weeks and it ay gone out yet."

Aynuk: "Me and the missus 'ad a bit of a difference last night. She wanted to go to the pictures and I was determined to go to the pub."

Ayli: "What was the film like?"

Ayli: "My missus is nowt but a liar."

Aynuk: "Ow dun yo know?"

Ayli: "Cos 'er said 'er went out last night wi' Rosey."

Aynuk: "So what?"

Ayli: "I went out last night with Rosey."

Aynuk answered a knock at the door. A chap stood there smiling.

"I'm collecting for the old folks' home," he said.

"'Ang on a minute," said Aynuk, "yo can tek the mother-in-law."

Ayli: "Wot yo got in that bag our Aynuk?"

Aynuk: "Oranges, mate."

Ayli: "If I can guess how many yo've got will yer give me one?"

Aynuk: "If yo'm right I'll gi' yer both on 'em."

Ayli: "Five?"

56

Aynuk was fed up with frozen food and asked the missus to cook an old fashioned meal for a change. So she went out and bought a tin of meat, a tin of peas, a tin of carrots . . . !

Aynuk says his missus won't divorce him because it would upset her to see him happy!

A chap fell down in the road. Another, helping him to his feet, asked:

"Have you vertigo?"

"No," the chap replied, "only just round the corner."

Ayli had to go into hospital and the first thing they did was give him a good bath. When he was dry he said, "I've bin dreadin' that operation fer years but it wor too bad!"

Ayli went to the opticians complaining of bad eyesight. The optician took him into the street and pointed up at the sky.

"What's that object up there?" he asked.

"That's the sun ay it?" said Ayli.

"Well," asked the optician, "how much further do you want to see?"

You can't fool Black Country kids. A teacher was testing the intelligence of his class.

"Give me a number," he shouted.

"38," called one lad. The teacher wrote 83 on the blackboard.

"Give me another," he shouted.

"54" came the reply. The teacher wrote 45.

"One more" he shouted.

"99, ' called Tommy, "and see if yo con muck about wi' that!"

"You are a compulsive pickpocket and I hereby fine you fifty pounds for your offences," said the judge.

"Well I ay got the money," replied the criminal, "but if yo could just let me 'ave ten minutes in the gallery . . .!"

58

Aynuk was at the quizzes again.

"With what do you connect the name Baden-Powell?"

Ayli scratched his head before answering, "I ay sure but I think they call it an' 'yphen."

Ayli went in to see the gaffer about a rise.

"Yo ought to gi' me a rise 'cos I've got three companies after me," he said.

"And who might they be?" enquired his gaffer.

"Well," said Ayli, "there's the Gas Board, the Water Board and the Electricity Board for a start."

Aynuk: "The missus is mad about that Burt Reynolds. She says 'e sends 'er."

Ayli: "Oh ar."

Aynuk: "Ar, she says as I send 'er too . . . only not so fer."

Aynuk saw Ayli digging a hole in his garden.

"Where am yo going to put all that soil, Ayli," he asked.

"I'm going to dig another hole and bury it," said Ayli.

"But wo yo 'ave some soil left over?"

"I ay that saft," says Ayli, "I'm diggin' this hole deeper."

When he was a kid Ayli used to play truant from school for two days every week. Then he found out that none of the other kids went to school on Saturdays and Sundays either.

Aynuk: "I heard on the radio as there's talk of another strike."
Ayli: "Ar, the missus says if I were a proper mon I'd gerra job and goo on strike too!"

Judge to accused in the dock before him, "This is the second time in two years that you have appeared before this court accused of stealing overcoats. Have you anything to say?"

"Ar," came the reply, "they doh last forever yo know!"

Aynuk: "I told the missus that I was at me wits' end."
Ayli: "Wot did 'er say?"
Aynuk: "Er said I day 'ave to travel very far."

60

BLACK COUNTRY DUCK

"'E's allus like this just afore Christmas!"

"Yo'm allus talkin' about your car, your home and your garden. Why cor yo learn to say 'our'! Now what am yo lookin' for in the wardrobe?"

"Our trousers."

Aynuk and Ayli were walking along the canal towpath.

"I bet as I con throw yo across the cut to the other side," said Ayli.

"I bet yo a fiver yo cor," argued Aynuk.

So Ayli grabbed Aynuk by the arm and after swinging him round a couple of times he flung him straight into the cut.

"Yo owe me a fiver," shouted Aynuk as he swam to the edge.

"I doh," said Ayli, "I day say as I could do it fust time."

The little boy stretched across the table trying to reach the cakes.

"'Aven't yo gorra tongue?" his mother scolded.

"Ar," said the lad, "but it ay long enough."

Aynuk has been a bit upset of late. Seems that he'd been on the dole for ages and he was just getting on his feet when he got a job.

62

Ayli: "I've gorra problem wi' me motor."

Aynuk: "Wots the trouble, mate."

Ayli: "Water in the carburettor."

Aynuk: "We'll soon get that fixed, where's yer motor?"

Ayli: "They're just fishin' it out of the river."

A Black Countryman had applied for a job and had to sign an application form.

"I cor write so I'll have to mek a cross,' he said.

"That's fine, but why two crosses," asked the interviewer.

"Oh," said the applicant, "the second one stands for 'Ph.D.'"

Aynuk and Ayli were in a museum and were fascinated by some of the old pottery.

"Yo know," said Ayli, "that vase over there is one thousand years and three months old."

"'Ow con yer tell the exact date," queried Aynuk.

"Easy," replied Ayli, "when I cum three months ago they told me it were one thousand years old then."

Aynuk had been sorting through all the household bills and after examining his wallet he turned to his missus and said, "Yo'll be pleased to know as we've cum to the bridge as we said we'd cross when we cum to it."

A lady was being asked questions for a record card to keep some computer happy.
  "Name?"
  "Brown."
  "With an 'e'?"
  "No, I cum on me own. Me 'usband is at 'ome."

Aynuk was down at the butchers and was mekin' sure that he didn't get a tough piece of meat. After much searching the butcher felt sure he'd found the right joint.
  "'Ere we are, as tender as a woman's 'eart."
  "In that case," said Aynuk, "gi' us a pound of sausage."

The language of the Black Country is aptly summed up in the words of the irate lady. (And this has been said above once by more than one.)
  "It's the milkmon, 'e's bin an' gone an' ay cum agen!"

64

Aynuk: "Why does a surgeon wear a mask when he does an operation?"

Ayli: "So that they wo' recognise 'im if 'e meks a mess of it."

Aynuk and Gertie had been walking out for a long time. She was hoping that he would propose marriage and one evening as they sat on a park bench in the moonlight she gazed lovingly at Aynuk who was staring intently into space.

"Tell me, Aynuk," said Gertie, "is it me yer thinkin' of?"

"I was just wondering," said Aynuk

"Yes!" anticipated Gertie

"Well", said Aynuk, "I was just wondering if I could spit as fer as that lampost."

Ayli: "I've 'ad to stop in wi' the missus at night 'cos of the obscene telephone calls."

Aynuk: "That's terrible, mate."

Ayli: "Ar, but 'ers finally agreed to stop mekin' 'em!"